To: Mike
From: Tommy

Ephesians 3:14-19

(I can't say it any
better than Paul ☺)

Faith

Discovery House Publishers

Books, music, and videos that feed the soul with the Word of God

Box 3566 Grand Rapids, MI 49501

OSWALD
CHAMBERS

Faith

A Holy Walk

Compiled & edited by
JULIE ACKERMAN LINK

Faith: A Holy Walk
Copyright © 1999 by
Oswald Chambers Publications Association, Limited

Discovery House Publishers is affiliated with
RBC Ministries, Grand Rapids, Michigan 49512

Discovery House books are distributed to the trade
exclusively by Barbour Publishing, Inc.,
Uhrichsville, Ohio 44683

All Scripture quotations are from
the New King James Version.
Copyright © 1979, 1980, 1982 by
Thomas Nelson, Inc., Publishers.
Used by permission of Thomas Nelson Publishers.

Library of Congress Cataloging-in-Publication Data
Chambers, Oswald, 1874-1917.
    Faith: A Holy Walk / by Oswald Chambers.
      p.cm.
    ISBN 1-57293-53-5
    1. Christian life. 2. Faith. I. Title.

BV4501.2.C463   1999
234'.23--dc21

                              99-046084
                              CIP

Printed in the United States of America
99 00 01 02 03 04 05 / RRD / 10 9 8 7 6 5 4 3 2 1

CONTENTS

INTRODUCTION

THE way some people talk, you could get the idea that faith is nothing more than a spiritualized form of wishful thinking. "Just Believe" is a popular slogan that decorates everything from sweatshirts to wall hangings to Christmas cards and ornaments. But the kind of faith those two words advocate has more to do with the mystical power of positive thinking than with anything God ever said on the subject.

Although it doesn't do much good to talk back to a slogan, someone ought to ask, "Believe what?" Believe that God will repay money we foolishly borrow? Believe that God will neutralize the consequences of all our bad choices? Believe that God will give us the car, career, or spouse of our dreams if we promise to behave in a certain way?

Contrary to much of what we hear today, faith is not convincing ourselves that we have God's stamp of approval on our plans; it's believing that God's plans are better than ours.

That's what Noah believed, and so at God's instruction he set about building a houseboat to save himself, his family, and a remnant of the animal kingdom from the flood God said was coming, even though Noah had never seen a drop of rain in his life.

That's what Abraham believed, and so at God's command he left the comfort and familiarity of home and headed across the desert for a place God said was better, even though Abraham had never seen it.

That's what Moses believed, and so by faith he refused the privileges rightfully his as the son of Egypt's ruler and identified himself instead with people God said He had chosen for Himself, even though they were still slaves belonging to Pharaoh.

Biblical faith is not about taking risks; it's about taking on the identity of Jesus. It's not about having the audacity to do what is foolish; it's about having the courage to do what is difficult. It's not about running in the dark; it's about walking in the light. It's not about believing what people say about God; it's simply believing what God says.

Faith Is Believing
What God Says
About the World

FAITH in God is a terrific venture in the dark; I have to believe that God is good in spite of all that contradicts it in my experience. It is not easy to say that God is love when everything that happens actually gives the lie to it. Everyone's soul represents some kind of battlefield. The point for each one is whether we will hang in and say, "Though things look black, I will trust in God."   — BFB

When I am surrounded by darkness,
do I see nothing or do I see God? Do
I consider darkness an opportunity
to rest or a reason to become restless?
What good reason might God have
for keeping me in the dark?

FAITH is praying with our eyes on God, not on the difficulties.   — GW

SOME of us are no good unless we are kept in the circumstances in which our convictions were formed, but God is constantly stirring up our nests so we may learn that a relationship with Christ is not altered in any circumstance. Logic or a vivid past experience can never take the place of personal faith in a personal God. It is easier to be true to a conviction formed in a vivid religious experience than to be true to Christ, because if I am true to Christ, my convictions will have to be altered. — JER

Do I make it a practice to fit my experience into the context of God's revealed Word? Or do I try to fit God's revealed Word into the context of my experience?

NEVER assume anything that has not been made yours by faith and the experience of life; it is presumptuous to do so. On the other hand, be ready to be considered foolish for proclaiming to others what is really yours.

— DI

EXPERIENCE is a gateway, not an end.
Beware of building your faith on experience.
You can never give another person that which
you have found, but you can make him long
for what you have.   — MUHH

*Do I live a spiritual life that causes
others to want to know the God I
love or do I lead a religious life
that causes others to hate the
god I follow?*

BE ruthless with yourself if you are given to
talking about the experiences you have had.
Faith that is sure of itself is not faith; faith that
is sure of God is the only faith there is.

                                      — MUHH

THE faith of many really spiritual Christians is eclipsed today, and the reason it is eclipsed is that they tried to remain true and consistent to the narrow confines of their experience instead of getting out into the light of God.

— PH

Do I consider experience to be a reward for faith or a means to faith? Do I consider behavior to be proof of faith or an expression of faith? Do I do good things to get God to love me or to show that I love Him? Which are more pleasing to God?

IN dealing with the life of Abraham as the Father of the faithful neither faith nor common sense must be our guide, but God Who unites both in the test tube of personal experience. To be guided by common sense alone is fanatical; both common sense and faith have to be brought into relation to God.   — NKW

ISAIAH called his people to exercise unshaken faith in God and in His deliverance, of which there seemed no likelihood. This profound truth runs all through God's Word. It is not faith when you trust in what you see; faith is trusting in what you don't see, hanging in to the God whose character you know though meantime there is no evidence that He is at work on your behalf.   — IS

What aspect of God's character is He proving to me in ways I cannot see? What is the invisible evidence of God's work in my life?

WHEN the baptism of the Holy Ghost came upon the early disciples it made them the living epistles of what they taught, and it is to be the same with us. Jesus Christ is always infinitely mightier than our faith, mightier than our experience, but our experience will be along the line of the faith we have in Him.

— PF

WE have no faith at all until it is proved through conflict. There are things in life that come out against our faith in God's goodness and justice. Are we going to remain steadfast in our faith in God until we see all that contradicts our common sense transfigured into exactly what our faith believes it should be?

— HSGM

Do I claim to have faith in areas where I've never had reason to doubt? Is this true faith or just absence of doubt? Do I claim to be victorious in areas where I've never been tempted to sin? Is this righteousness or arrogance?

THE greatest demand God makes of us is to believe that He is righteous when everything that happens goes against that faith.

— GW

THE acts of faith the writer of Hebrews refers to were not performed by astute-minded men and women who made defined statements about God. They were not tortured for convictions' sake, but for the sake of their faith. And God is training us to do what they did — to live a life of tenacious hold upon God in spite of everything that happens.   — HSGM

Am I tied down by my faith in earthly convictions or set free from earthly conditions by faith in heavenly promises?

MANY of us have no faith in God at all, but only faith in what He has done for us, and when these things are not apparent we lose our faith and say, "Why should this happen to me?"   — BFB

THE love of God! We have turned our back on the ocean of it and are looking for it out over barren colorless hills. We need converting again — turning round, and there basks the ocean's fullness, whose waves sparkle and ripple on fathomless deeps. We are too introspective today, we mourn and wonder, then, lifted on waves of feeling, we glow and say we love God. But again our feelings ebb and flow and we mourn. Christianity is not a thing of times and seasons, but of God and faith. — LG

What am I trying to get from human relationships that only God can provide? What am I waiting for God to give me which He has not promised and which I have no right to expect?

DRINK deep and full of the love of God and you will not demand the impossible from earth's loves. Then the love of wife and child, of husband and friend, will grow holier and healthier and simpler and grander.   — LG

THE average view of Christianity — that we only need to have faith and we are saved — is a stumbling block. How many of us care anything about being witnesses to Jesus Christ? How many of us are willing to spend every ounce of energy we have, every bit of mental, moral, and spiritual life for Jesus Christ? God has left us on earth, what for? To be saved and sanctified? No, to be working for Him.

— AUG

Am I a channel of God's blessing to others or only a consumer? Is God's goodness being multiplied and magnified in my life or hidden, hoarded, and devoured?

SPIRITUAL famine and dearth, if it does not start from sin, starts from dwelling entirely on the experience God gave me instead of on God who gave me the experience. When I plant my faith on the Lord Jesus my experiences don't make me conscious of them, they produce in me the life of a child.

— DI

WE all have faith in good principles, in good management, in good common sense, but who among us has faith in Jesus Christ? Physical courage is grand, moral courage is grander, but the man who trusts Jesus Christ in the face of the terrific problems of life is worth a whole crowd of heroes. — HG

Do I place more confidence in science than in Scripture? More trust in human legislation than in divine justice? More faith in good government than in a loving God?

IN the face of problems as they are, we see in Jesus Christ an exhibition of where our faith is to be placed — in a God whose ways we do not understand. — DI

JEREMIAH had to minister to a people who became worse and worse because he ministered to them. It is incorporated into us that we are to succeed for God. In the New Testament there is no such notion, only faithfulness to Jesus Christ. God has His own purposes which we do not know, and our purpose is to see that we remain steadfastly faithful to Him.

— JER

Is it my habit to continue doing
what I know is right even when I see
no results from my efforts? Am I
more likely to criticize or encourage
others who are doing right but not
yet reaping righteousness?

THE only recognition you will have in the eyes of the world as My disciples, says Jesus, is that "you will be hated for My name's sake." That is why we need to be knit together with those of like faith; and that is the meaning of the Christian Church. — AUG

EVERY time you venture out in the life of faith, you will find something in your common-sense circumstances that flatly contradicts your faith. Common sense is not faith, and faith is not common sense; they stand in the relation of the natural and the spiritual. Can you trust Jesus Christ where your common sense contradicts Him?   — MUHH

How often do I stop to think that what seems normal is not necessarily good? How often do I consider that the "sensible" thing to do is not always the right thing?

WHENEVER you meet with difficulties, whether they are intellectual, circumstantial, or physical, remain loyal to God. Don't compromise. If you do, everyone around you will suffer from your faithlessness, because you are disloyal to Jesus Christ and His way of looking at things.   — PH

DARKNESS comes by the sovereignty of
God. Are we prepared to let God do as He
likes with us — prepared to be separated from
conscious blessings? Until Jesus Christ is Lord,
we all have ends of our own to serve. Our
faith is real, but it is not yet permanent. God
is never in a hurry; if we wait, we shall see that
God is pointing out that we have not been
interested in Himself, but only in His blessings.   — MUHH

*Am I more interested in what God
can do for me than what He wants
to do in me? Do I believe that God
can change bitter circumstances
into sweet blessing? Am I
willing to let Him?*

TREASURE in heaven is faith that has been
tried (see Revelation 3:18). When we begin to
have fellowship with Jesus, immediately we
have to live the life of faith at all costs; it may
be bitter to begin with, but afterwards it is
ineffably and indescribably sweet.   — IYWB

A MAN of faith can go through tribulations which make you hold your breath as you watch him; he goes through things that would knock the wits out of us and make us give way to blasphemy and whimperings. He is not blind or insensitive, yet he goes through in marvelous triumph. What accounts for it? One thing only, the fact that behind it all is the love of God which is in Christ Jesus our Lord.

— SHL

In times of trouble do I open my mouth to complain or keep it shut to express my confidence in God? Do I trust God to sustain me through times of trouble or do I only expect Him to get me out of trouble?

YOU can shut the mouth of the man who has faith in God, but you cannot get away from the fact that he is being kept by God.

— SHL

EXPERIENCE is never the ground of my faith; experience is the evidence of my faith. Many of us have had a marvelous experience of deliverance from sin and of the baptism of the Holy Ghost, a real experience whereby we prove to our amazement every day that God has delivered us. Then comes the danger that we pin our faith to our experience instead of to Jesus Christ, and if we do, faith becomes distorted. — PF

Do I proclaim by my life, my thinking, and my faith in God that Jesus Christ is sufficient for every problem life can present and that there is no force too great for Him to cope with and overcome?

IF our faith is not living and active it is because we need reviving; we have a faith that is limited by certain doctrines instead of being "the faith of God." — PF

MOST of us get touchy with God when He does not back up our beliefs. Many of us, having lost our form of belief in God, imagine that we have thereby lost God, whereas we are in the throes of a conflict which ought to give birth to a realization of God more fundamental than any statement of belief.   — BFB

When my circumstances contradict my understanding of God do I pull away from Him in anger or move toward Him in eagerness to learn something new?

NEVER be afraid if your circumstances dispute what you have been taught about God; be willing to examine what you have been taught. To many, God is merely a theological statement, so when our religious forms of belief are swept away for a while, we say, "I have lost my faith in God." What has really happened is that we have lost faith in our statement of God, and we are on the way to finding God Himself.   — BFB

HOW much of our security and peace is the outcome of the civilized life we live, and how much is built up in faith in God? — JER

When I watch soldiers march off to war and see nations fighting for power, I wonder . . . Do I have more confidence in military might than in the mighty power of God? Would I be as confident about my faith if I lived in a nation that had fewer weapons and a weaker military?

EVERY time you venture out on the life of faith, you will come across something which seems to contradict what your faith in God says you should believe. Go through this trial of faith and lay up your confidence in God, not in your common sense, and you will gain much wealth in your heavenly account. The more you go through the trial of faith, the wealthier you will become in the heavenly regions. — SSM

Faith Is Believing

What God Says

About the Flesh

IN the early days of spiritual experience we walk more by sight and feelings than by faith. The comforts, the delights, the joys of contact are so exquisite that the very flesh itself tingles with the leadings of the cloudy pillar by day and the fiery pillar by night; but there comes a day when all that ceases.　　　　　　— CD

What am I doing today, while it is light, to prepare myself for future times of darkness? Do I know God well enough to follow Him even when my senses are unable to perceive Him?

THERE is a great difference between Christian experience and Christian faith. The danger of experience is that our faith is made to rest in it, instead of seeing that our experience is simply a doorway to God Himself.

　　　　　　— BFB

BECAUSE we cannot experience the foundations of Christian faith we are apt to discard them as unnecessary: they are more necessary than all the experiences which spring from them. To say, "You don't need theology to save a soul" is like saying, "What is the good of a foundation? What we want is a house." The good of the foundation is that storms cannot wreck the house built on a strong foundation (see Matthew 7:24–27). — HSGM

What is the foundation on which my faith stands? What pieces are missing? What places are weak? Where is it uneven or unbalanced? What repairs do I need to make?

WHAT hinders the purging of our perception is that we will build our faith on our experiences instead of on the God who gave us the experiences. My experience is the evidence of my faith, never the ground of it, and is meant to reveal to me a God who is bigger than any experience. — IS

AFTER we have been perfectly related to God in sanctification, our faith has to be worked out in reality. We will be scattered into inner desolations and made to know what internal death to God's blessings means. Are we prepared for this? It is not that we choose it, but that God engineers our circumstances so that we are brought there. Until we have been through that experience, our faith is bolstered by feelings and blessings. When we get there, no matter where God places us or what inner desolations we experience, we can praise God that all is well.   — MUHH

Does my faith depend on my feelings or on God's truth? On the blessings I receive from God or on His character being formed in my life?

EXPERIENCE is never the ground of our trust, it is the gateway to the One Whom we trust. The work of faith is not an explanation to our minds, but a determination on our part to obey God and to make a concession of our faith in His character.   — NKW

IF we construct our faith on our experience, we produce that most unscriptural type of holiness, an isolated life, with our eyes fixed on our own whiteness. If we do not base all our thinking on the presupposition of the Atonement, we shall produce a faith conscious of itself, hysterical and unholy, that cannot do the work of the world. Beware of the piety that has no presupposition of the Atonement, it is no use for anything but leading a sequestered life; it is useless to God and a nuisance to man.   — AHW

Is my faith so strong that it protects me from the challenges of the world or so weak that I protect it from all worldly challenges?

THE great need is not to do things, but to believe things. The Redemption of Christ is not an experience; it is the great act of God which He has performed through Christ, and I have to build my faith upon it.   — RTR

WE cannot have faith whenever we think we will. The Holy Spirit brings a word of Jesus to our remembrance and applies it to the circumstances we are in, and the point is, will we obey that particular word? We may have seen Jesus and known His power and yet never have ventured out in faith on Him.   — PF

Is my faith good for all circumstances, or do I turn it off and on for my own convenience? Does my faith make me more conscious of my own failures or only the failures of others? Does it cause me to witness about how God has changed me or to whine that He hasn't changed someone else?

TO say what God has done for you is testimony, but you have to preach more than you have experienced — more than anyone has ever experienced; you have to preach Jesus Christ, the Object of your faith.   — DI

THE call of God is like the call of the sea or of the mountains; no one hears these calls except the one who has the nature of the sea or of the mountains. And no one hears the call of God who has not the nature of God in him. It cannot be definitely stated what the call of God is to, because it is a call into a relationship with God Himself for His own purposes, and the test of faith is to believe that God knows what that purpose is. — NKW

Do I believe that God has a purpose for me? What is it? Am I doing it or am I waiting for God to explain it or give me some assurance as to its outcome?

WHEN we hear the call of God it is not for us to dispute with God, and arrange to obey Him if He will expound the meaning to us. As long as we insist on having the call expounded to us, we will never obey. If we insist on explanations before we obey, we put ourselves against His purpose. — NKW

THE call of God only becomes clear as we obey, never as we weigh the pros and cons and try to reason it out. The call is God's idea, not our idea, and only on looking back over the path of obedience do we realize what is the idea of God; God sanctifies memory.

— NKW

Am I willing to obey God in such matters as kindness, honesty, and generosity when I can't understand the reason for it? Which is more important to me: obedience or understanding? Which is more important to God?

IF we say, "I want to know why I should do this," it means we have no faith in God, but only sordid confidence in our own wits.

— NKW

THE forward look sees everything in God's perspective. Learn to take the long view of God and you will breathe His benediction among the squalid things that surround you. Paul was so identified with Jesus Christ that he had the audacity to say that what men saw in his life in the flesh was the very faith of the Son of God.   — PF

How well am I learning to identify with Jesus and to view my problems from His perspective? What ideas, attitudes, or behaviors are clouding my vision of God?

NEVER run away with the idea that you can do a thing or have an attitude of mind before God which no one else need know anything about. A man is what he is in the dark. Remain loyal to God and to His saints in private and in public, and you will find that not only are you counting on God, but that God is counting on you.   — PH

Faith Is Believing

What God Says

About the Devil

SATAN ever perverts what God says. Genesis 3:5 is one of the revelation facts concerning Satan: "For God knows that in the day you eat of it your eyes will be opened, and you will be like God, knowing good and evil." Remember, the characteristics of man's union with God are faith in God and love for Him. This union was the first thing Satan aimed at in Adam and Eve, and he did it by perverting what God had said.   — BP

*Am I an easy target for the devil's
lies or do I know enough about what
God says so that Satan can't deceive
me by twisting the truth?*

IN the case of Job, Satan goes the length of trying to pervert God's idea of man. That is an amazing revelation of the power of Satan! He is represented as presenting himself with the sons of God in the very presence of God and trying to pervert God's mind about Job. Satan is "the accuser of our brethren" (Revelation 12:10); he not only slanders God to us, but accuses us to God.   — BP

GOD never once makes His way clear to Job. God and Satan had made a battleground of Job's soul without Job's permission. Without any warning, Job's life is suddenly turned into desperate havoc, and God keeps out of sight, never giving any sign whatever to Job that He is around. The odds are desperately against God, and it looks as if the sneer of Satan will prove to be true; but God wins in the end, Job comes out triumphant in his faith in God, and Satan is vanquished.   — BFB

Is my heart tuned to God's frequency or Satan's? Do I sometimes believe that the only way to win is to use Satan's methods and strategies?

WE can develop in the heart life whatever we will; there is no limit to the possible growth. If we give ourselves over to meanness and to Satan, there is no end to the growth in devilishness; if we give ourselves over to God, there is no end to our growth in grace. Our Lord has no fear of the consequences when once the heart is open toward Him.   — BP

FAITH is implicit confidence in Jesus and in His faith. It is one thing to have faith in Jesus and another thing to have faith about everything for which He has faith. The apostle Paul not only had faith in Jesus as his Savior, but also the faith of Jesus (Galatians 2:20).　— PF

Is my faith at the beginning level
of trusting Jesus to save me in the
hereafter or at the advanced level of
trusting Jesus to defeat Satan in
the here and now?

THE faith that characterized Jesus characterized Paul as well. The identical faith that was in Jesus Christ, the faith that governed His life and which Satan could not break, was in him through identification with the death of Jesus.

— PF

FAITH must be tried, otherwise it is of no worth to God. Think of the dignity it gives to a man's life to know that God has put His honor in his keeping. Our lives mean more than we can tell; they mean that we are fulfilling some purpose of God about which we know nothing more than Job did. God's government of the world is not for material prosperity, but for moral ends, for the production of moral characters, in the sense of holy characters. Time is nothing to God. — PF

Is the soil of my faith more suitable for growing the vices Satan is planting or the virtues God is pruning?

NEVER run away with the idea that Satan is skeptical of all virtue; he knows God too well and human nature too well to have such a shallow skepticism; he is skeptical only of virtue that has not been tried. Faith untried is simply a promise and a possibility, which we may cause to fail; tried faith is the pure gold.

— PF

THE devil and all the great world forces cannot do a thing without God's permission. Today we so often emphasize the freedom of the human will that we forget the sovereignty of God. Consequently when we come up against the forces at work in the world we are paralyzed by fear and get into despair, which we need never do if we are built up in faith in God.

— IS

Do I live as if God or Satan has more power? When trouble comes, is my first response worship or worry? Does my presence in the world make Satan's job easier or more difficult?

IF I remain confident in God I lift the weight off lives in a way I shall never realize till I stand before Him. We have to pray that the enemy shall not exact upon the hearts and minds of God's children and make them slander Him by worry and anxiety. We are to hold off the exactings of Satan, not add to them.

— GW

THE one thing Satan tries to shake is our confidence in God. It is not difficult for our confidence to be shaken if we build on our experience; but if we realize that all we experience is but the doorway leading to the knowledge of God, Satan may shake that as much as he likes, but he cannot shake the fact that God remains faithful (see 2 Timothy 2:13).

— PSG

How is Satan trying to shake my confidence in God? Am I trembling in fear or standing firm in faith? When my faith is shaken, what am I trusting besides God?

IT is not our trust that keeps us; it is the God in whom we trust who keeps us. We are always in danger of trusting in our trust, believing our belief, having faith in our faith. All these things can be shaken; we have to base our faith on those things which cannot be shaken (see Hebrews 12:27).   — PSG

IT is easy to say God reigns, and then to see Satan, suffering, and sin reigning, and God apparently powerless. Belief in God must be tried before it is of value to God or to a child of His. It is the trial of our faith that makes us wealthy in God's sight.　　　　— PH

How much is my faith worth to God? Do the forces which Satan uses against it cause it to corrode like cheap metal or to shine like precious gold?

GOD is the only Being Who can stand the slander that arises because the devil and pain and sin are in the world. Stand true to the life hid with Christ in God and to the facts you have to face. You will have no answer intellectually, but your faith in God will be so unshakably firm that others will begin to see there is an answer they have never guessed.　　— PH

THE great point of Abraham's faith in God was that he was prepared to do anything for God. He was there to obey God, no matter what. Abraham was not a devotee of his convictions, or he would have slain Isaac and said that the voice of the angel was the voice of the devil. — MUHH

In what way has Satan crept into my convictions? Which of my beliefs about God are more important to me than God? Which of my religious convictions does Satan want me to keep in place of God?

IF you will remain true to God, God will lead you straight through every barrier into the inner chamber of the knowledge of Himself; but there is always this point of giving up convictions and traditional beliefs.

— MUHH

SELF-PITY is of the devil; if I go off on that line I cannot be used by God for His purpose in the world. I have "a world within the world" in which I live, and God will never be able to get me outside it because I have fear, not faith.

— MUHH

Why am I afraid to get close to God? What keeps me from believing that His purpose for me is good and that His love for me is perfect? Why do I persist in telling God what I want rather than in finding out what He wants me to have?

WHEN I stop telling God what I want, He can get me ready to do what He wants without hindrance. He can crumple me up or exalt me. He can do anything He chooses. He simply asks me to have implicit faith in Himself and in His goodness.

— MUHH

CERTAIN phases of the life of faith look so much like humbug that we are apt to grieve God's Spirit by our religious respectability in regard to them, and ecstasy is just one of those phases.
— NKW

Would I welcome or resist an encounter with God that led to an ecstatic emotional experience? Would I rather have an ecstatic experience with my own emotions than a genuine encounter with God?

ECSTASY is a state of mind that is marked by mental alienation from our surroundings, and our very consciousness is altered into excessive joy. These states are open gateways for God or for the devil. If they are worked up by thrills of our own seeking, they are of the devil; but when they come unsought in faithful performance of duties, they are the gateway into direct communication with God.
— NKW

THE life of faith is one in which we habitual-
ly work out that disposition through our eyes
and ears and tongue — through all the organs
of our body and in every detail of our life. We
have been identified with the death of Jesus
Christ; our whole life has been invaded by a
new spirit. We no longer have any connection
with the body of sin, that mystical body
which ultimately ends with the devil. We are
made part of the mystical Body of Christ by
sanctification.   — BP

Am I separating myself from sin?
Am I learning to love righteousness?
Am I becoming more like Jesus or
more like the world?

THERE is only one kind of holiness, and that
is the holiness of the Lord Jesus. There is only
one kind of human nature, and that is the
human nature of us all. And there is only one
kind of faith, and that is believing that Jesus
Christ, by means of His identification with
our human nature, can give us His disposition.
                                                            — BP

FAITH IS BELIEVING

WHAT GOD SAYS

ABOUT MY MIND

FAITH never knows where it is being led, but it loves and knows the One Who is leading. It is a life of faith, not of intellect and reason, but a life of knowing Who makes us "go." The root of faith is the knowledge of a Person, and one of the biggest snares is the idea that God is sure to lead us to success. — MUHH

How does my definition of success differ from God's? How does my definition of goodness differ from God's? Do I have the type of faith that gives me the courage to do the difficult things God wants me to do or the audacity to justify the easy things I want to do?

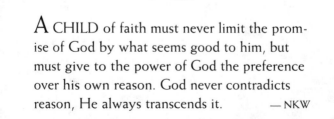

A CHILD of faith must never limit the promise of God by what seems good to him, but must give to the power of God the preference over his own reason. God never contradicts reason, He always transcends it. — NKW

ALONG with the craving to be right with God, there is also a deep resentment, born of our laziness, that we should be expected to understand these things, and the urgency all through the New Testament is that we should stir up our minds to search out these things, and build ourselves up on our most holy faith. We are called upon not only to be right in heart, but to be right in thinking. — BSG

In what areas has worldly reasoning corrupted my thinking? What carelessness do I allow in my life that causes my thinking to get out of align with God? What do I do to get it realigned?

IF we base our philosophy on reason, we shall produce a false philosophy; but if we base it on faith in God, we can begin to expound life rightly. — BFB

THE temper of mind is tremendous in its effects; it is the enemy that penetrates right into the soul and distracts the mind from God. There are certain tempers of mind in which we never dare indulge; if we do, we find they have distracted us from faith in God, and until we get back to the quiet mood before God, our faith in Him is nil, and our confidence in the flesh and in human ingenuity is the thing that rules.   — MUHH

What thoughts do I indulge in that distract me from God's perfect purpose? Do I put more effort into trying to get people to understand me or helping them to understand God?

ST. Augustine prayed, "O Lord, deliver me from this lust of always vindicating myself." That temper of mind destroys the soul's faith in God. "I must explain myself; I must get people to understand." Our Lord never explained anything; He left mistakes to correct themselves.
                                            — MUHH

EVERY time my program of belief is clear to my own mind, I come across something that contradicts it. Let me say I believe God will supply all my need, and then let me run dry, with no outlook, and see whether I will go through the trial of faith, or whether I will sink back to something lower.   — MUHH

In what ways has Satan deceived me into thinking that God's provisions are better than His presence? In what areas of life do I have more faith in common sense than I do in God? Have I learned anything from Eve or do I too believe that the knowledge of good and evil is better than innocence?

THE way the serpent beguiled Eve through his subtlety was by enticing her away from personal faith in God to depend on her reason alone. Confusion comes when we are consistent to our convictions instead of to Christ.   — GW

THE element of discipline in the life of faith must never be lost sight of, because only by means of the discipline are we taught the difference between the natural interpretation of what we call good and what God means by good.   — NKW

What discipline has God used in my life to show me how my idea of goodness differs from His? Am I more likely to give grudging assent to God's way with me or wholehearted agreement?

WE have to be brought to the place of hearty agreement with God as to what He means by good, and we only reach it by the trial of our faith, never by a stoical effort, such as saying, "Well, I must make up my mind that this is God's will, and that it is best."   — NKW

PETER does not say "give an explanation," but "a reason for the hope that is in you" (1 Peter 3:15). Be ready to say what you base your hope on. Faith is deliberate confidence in the character of God Whose ways you cannot understand at the time. Faith is not a conscious thing, it springs from a personal relationship and is the unconscious result of believing someone.

— FR

Do I have enough confidence in God's character to believe what He says even when it seems to contradict what I see?

MY faith is manifested in what I do, and I am able to explain slowly where I put my confidence. The faith that swallows is not faith, but credulity or fatalism. I have to get a grasp of the thing in my intellect, but that is second, not first.

— FR

ARE we going to obey our Lord or take the ordinary common-sense way of moral decisiveness? Are we going to stand fast in the faith, or take the easier way of decision without deliberation? To think along this line will give the death blow to the dangerous method of making principles out of our Lord's statements. To do that, we do not need to maintain a detached life with Him; all we need is to gain an intellectual grasp of His principles and endeavor to live our life in accordance with them.

— FR

In what ways does a corrupt conscience make life easier? Am I willing to submit my intellect to the revealed will of God and refuse to let it be corrupted, even though it will make life more difficult?

FAITH cannot be intellectually defined; faith is the capacity to see God behind everything, the wonder that keeps you an eternal child.

— HSGM

PAUL gives the rule for the thinking life of the Christian. Have we ever given our brains the task of concentrated thinking along that line? "Finally, brethren, whatever things are true, whatever things are noble, whatever things are just, whatever things are pure, whatever things are lovely, whatever things are of good report, if there is any virtue and if there is anything praiseworthy — meditate on these things" (Philippians 4:8).　　　— BSG

How much time do I spend each day thinking about things that are not honest, pure, and lovely? How might my life be better if I were to discipline my mind to focus on love, not hate; purity, not perversion; truth, not lies?

WE are called upon not only to be right in heart, but to be right in thinking. When we have become personally related to Jesus Christ we have to do the thing that is in our power to do, that is, think aright.　　　— BSG

IT is because we will not bring every thought into captivity to the obedience of Christ that all the perplexities are produced regarding methods of thinking which look like Christianity — strands are taken out of Jesus Christ's teaching, the Bible is exploited to agree with certain principles, but The Truth, Our Lord Jesus Christ, is ignored.   — BSG

In what ways do I exploit Scripture to make it agree with my ideas? In what ways do I exalt Scripture by allowing it to change my thinking? What thoughts do I allow to run loose in my mind? What is my strategy for bringing them under control?

WE have to get out of the old pagan way of guiding ourselves by our heads and get into the Christian way of being guided by faith in a personal God, whose methods are a perpetual contradiction to our every preconceived notion.   — DI

IF we base our thinking on principles instead of on a Person we shall go wrong, no matter how devout or honest we are. The one great Truth to keep steadfastly before us is the Lord Jesus Christ; He is the Truth. Only the whole truth is The Truth, any part of the truth may become an error. If you have a ray of light on The Truth never call it the whole truth; follow it up and it will lead you to the central Truth, the Lord Jesus Christ. — BSG

Which piece of God's truth do I focus on most often? How might this be distorting my view of God? Which aspect of truth am I most passionate about? How might this be distorting my view of myself and the world?

FAITH is more than an attitude of the mind; it is the complete, passionate, earnest trust of our whole nature in the Gospel of God's grace as it is presented in the Life and Death and Resurrection of our Lord Jesus Christ. — OBH

BELIEVING does not make a man redeemed; believing enables him to realize that he is redeemed. To any man who thinks, the basis of life is not reason, but Redemption. The miracle of the work of God is performed when he places himself on the "It is finished" side of the Cross. — BSG

If belief is just the doorway to salvation and sanctification, not the main living area, how much more of the house do I have yet to discover and enjoy?

A SPIRITUALLY minded Christian has to go through the throes of a total mental readjustment; it is a God-glorifying process, if a humbling one. People continually say, "How can I have more faith?" You may ask for faith, but you will never have faith apart from Jesus Christ. You can't pump up faith out of your own heart. — PF

IF we are going to find out the secrets of the world we live in, we must work at it. God does not encourage laziness. He has given us instruments whereby we are able to explore this universe and we do it entirely by intellectual curiosity; but when we come to the domain which Jesus Christ reveals, no amount of studying or curiosity will avail. — SSM

How do I want God to reveal Himself to me? What has He not yet shown me that I need to know? Do I sit around grumbling that God hasn't revealed Himself to me in a particular way, or do I spend time getting to know Him in the places where He has revealed Himself?

WE cannot see God or taste God. We cannot get at Him by our senses at all, so common sense is apt to say there is nothing other than this universe. — SSM

IF a man has lost belief in his beliefs, it does not follow therefore that he has lost faith in God. Many a man has been led to the frontiers of despair by being told he has backslidden, whereas what he has gone through has revealed that he believes in his beliefs, not in God. — BFB

Which is more important to me: to have God conform to my thoughts about Him or to conform myself to His way of thinking? Which is more important to God: to have other Christians agree with me or with Him? When believers disagree, who wins?

No quarrel is as bitter as a religious quarrel. If God can be summed up in a phrase, then there is the ban of finality about the view: "What I say is God." And this is the essential nature of religious tyranny. — BFB

THE key to life is not a statement of faith in God, nor an intellectual conception of God, but a personal relationship to Him. God Himself is the key to the riddle of the universe. When we take a scientific explanation as the key and leave out God, we only succeed in finding another lock.　　　　— BFB

What belief do I have that prevents me from having an intimate relationship with God?

EVERYTHING we take to be the key to a problem is apt to be another lock. For instance, the atomic theory was thought to be the key to the universe; then it was discovered that the atom itself was composed of electrons, and each electron was found to be a universe of its own, and that theory became a lock and not a key. Everything that man attempts as a simplification of life, other than a personal relationship to God, turns out to be a lock.　　　　— BFB

ALL certainty brings death to something.
When we have faith in a certain belief, we kill
God in our lives, because we do not believe
Him, we believe our beliefs about Him. The
helplessness of professional religion is that
there is no room for surprise. We tie God up
in His laws and in denominational doctrines
and orders of services. Consequently we do
not see God at all.   — LG

*What is the most troubling problem
in my life right now? How might it
be related to a faulty belief in God
which I refuse to give up?*

WE have to learn how to "go out" of everything — out of convictions, out of creeds, out
of experiences, out of everything — until so
far as our faith is concerned, there is nothing
between us and God.   — LG

THE problem all through the Book of Job is that Job's creed and his implicit faith in God do not agree, and it looks as if he is a fool to hang in to his belief in God. In the last chapter, we see everything rehabilitated, put back into rank, by means of Job's personal relationship to God. The basis of things must always be found in a personal relationship to a personal God, never in thinking or feeling.   — BFB

What faulty belief is keeping me from seeing the work God is doing in my life and in the world? What unhealthy desire is keeping me from doing the work of God in the world?

IF I am a devotee of a creed, I will not see God unless He comes along that line.   — FR

INTELLECT is never first in spiritual life. We are not born again by thinking about it, we are born again by the power of God. Intellect comes second both in nature and in grace. The things we can express intellectually are the things that are old in our experience; the things that are recent and make us what we are, we cannot define. A man's beliefs are the effect of his being a Christian, not the cause of it.   — HSGM

Do I give credit to my own intellect for my understanding of God? Is my faith a combination of intellect and experience? If so, how would it survive if I were deprived of both?

THE love of God is not revealed by intellectual discernment; it is a spiritual revelation. The ups and downs we experience are because we build not on faith but on feeling, not on the finished work of Christ but on our own work and effort and experience.   — LG

IF we really believed Jesus what a mighty difference there would be in us! We would trust
His Mind instead of our own; we would stop
being "amateur providences" over other lives,
and we would be fit to do our twenty-four
hours work like no one else.   — BE

*How does the thinking of Jesus
differ from my own? Which of His
thoughts am I most afraid of? What
keeps me from agreeing with Him?
What power over others am I
afraid of losing?*

THE basis of spiritual construction is implicit
faith in Jesus Christ. If I stake all on His astute
Mind I will find I have struck bedrock. The
majority of us only believe in Jesus Christ as
far as we can see by our own wits.   — BE

WE begin by saying, "I know that God is love, that He is just and holy and true"; then we come up against facts that flatly contradict what we said we believed. Are we going to succumb to pessimistic moods of intellect?

— PH

What circumstances make me doubt God's goodness? What facts make me doubt God's truthfulness? What feelings make me doubt God's power?

IF we try to answer the problems of this world by intellectual or scientific methods we shall go mad, or else deny that the problems exist. Never say that there is no such thing as death or sin or pain. Jesus Christ makes us open our eyes and look at these things.

— PH

A CREED is the ordered exposition of the Christian faith, an attempt to explain the faith you have, not the thing that gives you the Christian faith.

— FR

Am I more likely to rely on religious creeds for assurance that God is good or on religious feelings for evidence that He loves me? Why are both of these dangerous?

RELIGIOUS creeds are the most mature effort of the human intellect on the inside, not on the outside. Churches blunder when they put the creed as the test on the outside, and they produce parrots who mimic the thing.

— FR

WE shall not think of our Lord as a Savior if we look at Him in the light of our own minds, because no natural man imagines he needs to be saved. Do we make room in our faith for the impossible along the line of the supernatural? Or have we reduced our religion to such common-sense platitudes that there is no need for Jesus to have lived at all?   — PH

Faith Is Believing

What God Says

About my Heart

THE Christian life simply reconstructs the reasonings from the common-sense facts of natural life, preparing the way for that walk in faith that fears nothing because the heart is blazing with the love of God. — CD

Does my heart blaze with love for God or smolder with religious sentimentality? Can I hear the beat of God's heart in the accompaniment of a drum or only an organ? Do I truly desire God, or do I just want my favorite religious tradition?

FAITH is not an action of the mind, nor of the heart, nor of the will, nor of the sentiment, it is the centering of the entire man in God. — CD

IT appears as if God were sometimes most unnatural; we ask Him to bless our lives and bring benedictions, and what immediately follows turns everything into actual ruin. The reason is that before God can make the heart into a garden of the Lord, He has to plow it, and that will take away a great deal of natural beauty. — CD

Is the garden of my heart in the plowing, planting, or reaping stage? Am I allowing God to complete His work or am I always trying to pull up what He has sown so I can plant what I want to grow?

IF we interpret God's designs by our desires, we will say He gave us a scorpion when we asked an egg and a serpent when we asked a fish, and a stone when we asked for bread. But our Lord indicates that such thinking and speaking is too hasty; it is not born of faith or reliance on God. — CD

IF I try to describe to my own heart a be-
reaved home and let the sorrow of it weigh
with me, instantly my faith in God is gone; I
am so overcome with sympathy and feeling
for them that my prayer is nothing more than
a wail of sympathy before God. The telepathic
influence of my mind on another, whether I
speak or not, is so subtle that the prince of
this world will use it to prevent my getting
hold of God.   — GW

*Do I love to speak truth or do I just
love to speak? Do I speak to bless
others or to get them to bless me?
Does my compassion build
confidence in God or create
dependency on me?*

IT is righteous behavior that brings blessing
on others, and the heart of faith sees that God
is working things out well.   — PSG

CHRISTIANITY takes all the emotions, all the dangerous elements of human nature, the things which lead us astray, all feelings and excitabilities, and makes them into one great power for God. Other religions either cut out dangerous emotions altogether or base too much on them. The tendency is in us all to say, "You must not trust in feelings." Perfectly true, but if your religion is without feeling, there is nothing in it.   — BE

Do I deny my emotions because I
fear their power or do I engage their
power because I fear God? Do my
emotions fuel my life or steer it?

IF you are living a life right with God, you will have feeling, most emphatically so, but you will never run the risk of basing your faith on feelings. The Christian is one who bases his whole confidence in God and His work of grace, then the emotions become the beautiful ornament of the life, not the source of it. — BE

FEARS are facts. There is a danger in saying that because a thing is wrong, it does not exist. Fear is a genuine thing; without it there is no courage. The courageous man is the one who overcomes his fear. There are things in life that make us hold our breath; then in faith we look on to the end. — HSGM

What makes me fearful? What opportunity for exercising faith and developing courage lies within each fear? Is my faith strong enough to survive humiliation or is it only good when I'm getting recognition?

IF you stand for God's truth you are sure to experience reproach, and if once you open your mouth to vindicate yourself, you lose everything you were on the point of gaining. That is the test of a Christian, the power to descend until you are looked upon as absolute refuse and you have not a word to say any more than your Lord had. In that condition, see that your faith in God does not fail. — JER

THE stronghold of the Christian faith is joy *of* God not joy *in* God. It is a great thing for a man to have faith in the joy of God, to know that nothing alters the fact of God's joy. God reigns and rules and rejoices, and His joy is our strength. The miracle of the Christian life is that God can give a man joy in the midst of external misery, a joy which gives him power to work until the misery is removed. Joy is different from happiness, because happiness depends on what happens. There are elements in our circumstances we cannot help, joy is independent of them all. — HSGM

Do I spend more time chasing the world's idea of happiness or resting in God's idea of joyfulness?

IT is not faith to believe that God is making things work together for good unless we are up against things that are ostensibly working for bad. — HSGM

THE nature of faith is that it must be tested; and the trial of faith does not come in fits and starts, it goes on all the time. The one thing that keeps us right with God is the great work of His grace in our hearts. All the prophets had to take part in something they did not understand, and the Christian has to do the same. — IS

Faith Is Believing

What God Says

About my Soul

IT is possible to preach and to encourage our own souls and to appear to have a very strong faith, while in actual circumstances we do not stand fast at all, but rather prove what Herbert Spencer said to be true, that people think like pagans six days a week and like Christians the remaining day. Consequently in the actual things of life we decide as pagans, not as Christians at all.   — FR

Do I spend more time feeding my body or my soul? Which receives the more nourishing meals? Am I able to feed myself spiritually or do I eat only when other believers feed me?

THE saint is to be consistent to the Divine life within him, not to a logical principle. A fanatic is concerned not about God but about proving his own little fanatical ideas. It is a danger to us all. It is easier to be a fanatic than a faithful soul, because there is something amazingly humbling, particularly to our religious conceit, in being loyal to God.   — NKW

GOD does not ignore feelings and senses;
He elevates them. The first effort of the soul
toward bringing the body into harmony with
the new disposition is an effort of faith. The
soul has not yet got the body under way,
therefore in the meanwhile feelings have to be
discounted. — BP

Is my soul in harmony with God?
Are my senses in harmony with my
soul? What am I doing to make
peace between them? What forces are
working to keep them at war?

WHEN the new disposition enters the soul,
the first steps have to be taken in the dark, by
faith, without feeling; but as soon as the soul
gains control, all bodily organs are brought
into harmony. — BP

DESPAIR is always the gateway of faith. So many of us get depressed about ourselves, but when we get to the point where we are not only sick of ourselves, but sick to death, then we shall understand what the Atonement of the Lord Jesus Christ means. It will mean that we come to Him without the slightest pre-tense, without any hypocrisy, and say, "Lord, if You can make anything of me, do it," and He will do it. — HG

Have I gone through the gateway of despair or am I still sitting outside trying to make myself into something God will someday be proud of?

THE Lord can never make a saint out of a good man, He can only make a saint out of three classes of people — the godless man, the weak man, and the sinful man, and no one else, and the marvel of the Gospel of God's grace is that Jesus Christ can make us what He wants us to be. — HG

WHENEVER I become certain of my creeds, I kill the life of God in my soul, because I cease to believe in God and believe in my belief instead. All through the Bible the realm of the uncertain is the realm of joy and delight; the certainty of belief brings distress. Certainty of God means uncertainty in life; while certainty in belief makes us uncertain of God. Certainty is the mark of the common-sense life; gracious uncertainty is the mark of the spiritual life, and they must both go together.

— LG

Am I willing to be uncertain in my beliefs about God so that I can be certain of Him? Is my faith an excuse for weakness or the source of strength?

WHENEVER faith is starved in your soul it is because you are not in contact with Jesus; get in contact with Him and lack of faith will go in two seconds.

— PF

THERE is sufficient indication that when Adam's spirit, soul, and body were united in perfect faith and love to God, his soul was the medium through which the marvelous life of the Spirit of God was brought down. The very image of God was brought down into his material body, and it was clothed in an inconceivable splendor of light until the whole man was in the likeness of God. — BP

Has my soul been united with God through belief in His Son and the work of His Spirit or am I holding back because I still believe that Satan has something good to offer me?

SATAN was the originator of sin; Adam was not. But the moment man placed his faith in the devil and disobeyed God, the connection with God was shut off, and spirit, soul, and body tumbled into death that instant. — BP

Faith Is Believing
What God Says
About the Father

FAITH is not that I see God, but that I know God sees me; that is good enough for me, I will run out and play — a life of absolute freedom.
                                                              — NKW

Do I spend more time living in fearfulness because I can't see God or in freedom because I know that He sees me? Do I have confidence in the quiet aspects of His character or only in the visible displays of His power?

FAITH is unbreakable confidence in the Personality of God, not only in His power. There are some things over which we may lose faith if we have confidence in God's power only. There is so much that looks like the mighty power of God that is not. We must have confidence in God over and above everything He may do, and stand in confidence that His character is unsullied.
                                                              — IYWA

BEWARE of the tendency of asking the way when you know it perfectly well. Take the initiative, stop hesitating, and take the first step. Be resolute when God speaks, act in faith immediately on what He says, and never revise your decisions. If you hesitate when God tells you to do a thing, you endanger your standing in grace. Take the initiative, take it yourself, take the step with your will now, make it impossible to go back. Burn your bridges behind you — "I will write that letter"; "I will pay that debt." Make the thing inevitable.   — MUHH

Am I waiting for God to
increase my faith so that I'll have
the courage to obey, or am I asking
God for the courage to obey so that
He can increase my faith?

GOD does not give faith in answer to prayer: He reveals Himself in answer to prayer, and faith is exercised spontaneously.   — DI

GOD knew when He told Abraham to offer up Isaac for a burnt offering that Abraham would interpret it to mean he was to kill his son. God can only reveal His will according to the state of a man's character and his traditional belief. Abraham had to be brought to the last limit of the tradition he held about God before God could give him its right meaning. Abraham had to have his faith purified, to have it stripped of every tradition he held until he stood face to face with God and understood His mind. — IS

How has God purified my faith?
What traditions am I holding onto
that are not true to God's character?
What do they say about my
own character?

THE strength of life is not in the certainty that we can do the thing, but in the perfect certainty that God will. — LG

GOD sometimes allows you to get into a place of testing where your own welfare would be the right and proper thing to consider if you were not living a life of faith; but if you are, you will joyfully waive your right and leave God to choose for you. This is the discipline by means of which the natural is transformed into the spiritual by obedience to the voice of God. — MUHH

Am I more likely to believe that God's will is what I think is good for me or what God says is good for the world?

TO be so much in contact with God that you never need to ask Him to show you His will is to be nearing the final stage of your discipline in the life of faith. When you are rightly related to God, it is a life of freedom and liberty and delight; you are God's will, and your decisions are His will for you unless He checks. You decide things in perfect delightful friendship with God, knowing that if your decisions are wrong He will always check; when He checks, stop at once. — MUHH

THE great enemy of the life of faith in God
is not sin, but the good which is not good
enough. The good is always the enemy of the
best. Many of us do not go on spiritually
because we prefer to choose what is right
instead of relying on God to choose for us.
We have to learn to walk according to the
standard which has its eye on God.   — MUHH

*What seemingly good thing do I
insist on keeping in my life that may
be hindering God from giving
me His best?*

AS soon as you begin to live the life of faith
in God, fascinating and luxurious prospects
will open up before you, and these things are
yours by right; but if you are living the life of
faith you will exercise your right to waive your
rights, and let God choose for you.   — MUHH

A MAN who has faith in God is easily ridiculed. Then when he comes out into the sun people say, "What a cunning man he was; look how he worked it all out." We would rather credit man with an intelligence he never possessed than credit God with any intelligence at all.

— IS

Am I more likely to give credit
to God for what He has done or to
take credit myself for what
God is doing?

WE lose faith in God when we are hurt in the physical domain and God does not do what we want; we forget that He is teaching us to rely on His love. Watch some people and you will wonder how a human being can support such anguish; yet instead of being full of misery, they are the opposite; they seem to be held by a power that baffles all human intelligence, to have a spiritual energy we know nothing of.

— SHL

THE Christian faith affirms the existence of a personal God Who reveals Himself. Pseudo-Christianity departs from this. We are told we cannot know anything at all about God — we do not know whether He is a personal Being; we cannot know whether He is good. The Christian revelation is that God is a personal Being and He is good. By "good," I mean morally good. Test all beliefs about God by that; do they reveal clearly that God is good and that all that is moral and pure and true and upright comes from God?   — BE

What keeps me from believing that God is good? What keeps me from believing that He wants a relationship with me?

THERE are those who have maintained their faith in God, and the only language they can use to express it is, "I know God is God, even though hell seems on top all round."   — GW

WE are in danger of forgetting that we cannot do what God does, and that God will not do what we can do. We cannot save ourselves nor sanctify ourselves; God does that. And God will not give us good habits, He will not give us character, He will not make us walk aright. We have to do all that ourselves; we have to work out the salvation God has worked in us. — RTR

*Am I waiting for God to do
something that He expects me to do?
Am I trying to do something for
myself that only God can do?*

WE know that the character of God is noble and true and right, and any authority from God is based not on autocracy or mere blind power, but on worthiness which everything in me recognizes as worthy. Therefore I submit.

— BFB

DIVINE forgiveness is part of the unsearchable riches that are ours through Redemption. Because we do not realize the miracle of God's forgiveness we remain feeble in faith and thus evade the enormous demands faith makes on us. We talk glibly about forgiving when we have never been injured; when we are injured we know that it is impossible, apart from God's grace, for one human being to forgive another. When God forgives, He says, "I have blotted out, like a thick cloud, your transgressions, and like a cloud, your sins" (Isaiah 44:22). A cloud cannot be seen when it is gone.

— PH

Whom would I be obligated to forgive if I were to become stronger in my faith? Do I cling to my right to anger and hatred as a way of avoiding nearness to God?

BY the preaching of the Gospel God creates what was never there before — faith in Himself on the ground of the Redemption.

— DI

THE time of stress when there is no vision, no insight, no sensing of the presence of God is the time to stand firm in faith in God, and God will do all the rest. Keep true to God and your development in God's plan is certain.

— JER

Is God quiet? Then why don't I follow his cue and remain silent rather than scream for attention? Is God still? Then why don't I follow His example and stay put rather than fly into a flurry of activity?

GOD did not give a progressive revelation of Himself through the Old Testament; the people progressively grasped the revelation, and that is very different.

— IS

THE very nature of faith is that it must be tried. Faith is not rational, therefore it cannot be worked out on the basis of reason; it can only be worked out on the implicit line by living obedience. Faith must prove itself by the inward concession of its dearest objects, and in this way be purified from all traditional and fanatical ideas and misconceptions.   — NKW

If God took away the person I love most dearly, would I still believe He is loving? If God took away the talent I do the best, would I still believe He is sovereign? If God removed me from the place where I am appreciated the most, would I still believe He is good?

THE Bible does not deal with the domain of common-sense facts, we get at those by our senses; the Bible deals with the world of revelation facts which we only get at by faith in God.   — LG

WHEN God calls us He does not tell us along the line of our natural senses what to expect; God's call is a command that asks us, that means there is always a possibility of refusal on our part. Faith never knows where it is being led, it knows and loves the One Who is leading.

— NKW

How often do I doubt God because
He asks me to do something difficult?
How often do I disobey God because
I give too much consideration to
"tomorrow"?

WHEN God's call comes, I learn to do actively what He tells me and take no thought for the morrow.

— NKW

THE bedrock of our Christian faith is the unmerited, fathomless marvel of the love of God exhibited on the Cross of Calvary, a love we never can and never shall merit. Paul says this is the reason we are more than conquerors in all these things, super-victors, with a joy we would not have but for the very things which look as if they are going to overwhelm us.

— MUHH

*Do I enjoy spending time with God
or do I expect to receive enjoyment
as a reward for spending time
with Him?*

THE stronghold of the Christian faith is the joy *of* God, not my joy *in* God. . . . God reigns and rules and rejoices, and His joy is our strength.　　　　　　— RTR

IF we have faith at all it must be faith in Almighty God; when He has said a thing, He will perform it; we have to remain steadfastly obedient to Him. Are we learning to be silent unto God, or are we worrying Him with needless prayers? There is no more glorious opportunity than the day in which we live for proving in personal life and in every way that we are confident in God.   — PH

How does my life prove my confidence in God? Is my faith more like having hope that God will do what I want Him to do or having confidence that God will do what is best for His kingdom?

WHEN we pray we feel the blessing of God enwrapping us and for the time being we are changed; then we get back to the ordinary days and ways and the glory vanishes. The life of faith is not a life of mounting up with wings, but a life of walking and not fainting.

— MUHH

PRACTICAL work is nearly always a determination to think for myself, to take the pressure of forethought on myself: I see the need,
therefore I must do something. That is not the
effectual call of God, but the call of my sympathy with conditions as I see them. — NKW

*What perceived need of my own am
I devoting all my time and energy to
at the expense of meeting a more
important need that God sees and
wants me to address?*

IN the life of faith the pressure of forethought
is transferred to God. I have faith in God's
accountable rationality, not in my own. If I
have never heard the call of God, all I see is
the accountability that I can state to myself.

— NKW

WHEN you act in faith in God it is not logical proof that you are right that matters, but the certainty of the Divine approval, and this keeps you from seeking the approval of others.

— NKW

Do I measure my faith by whether or not I am able to get God to follow my plans or on whether or not He is able to get me to follow His? Do I measure my effectiveness by whether or not people are following me or whether or not I am following God?

WE have to make sure that we use our wits to assist us in worshiping God and carrying out His will, not in carrying out our own will and then asking God very piously to bless the concoction. Worship first and wits after.

— NKW

SPIRITUAL sulks arise because we want something other than God; we want God to give us something, to make us feel well, to give us wonderful insight into the Bible. That is not the attitude of a saint but of a sinner who is trying to be a saint, and who is coming to God to get things from Him. Unless we give to God the things we get from Him, they will prove our perdition. — NKW

*What conditions do I place on God
that keep me distant from Him?
What am I trying to get from God
as proof that He loves me?*

FAITH is not a bargain with God — I will trust You if. . . . We have to trust in God whether or not He sends us money, whether or not He gives us health. We must have faith in God, not in His gifts. — NKW

WE promise that we will do what God wants; we vow that we will remain true to Him, and we solemnly mark a text to this effect; but no human being can do it. We have to steadily refuse to promise anything and give ourselves over to God's promise, flinging ourselves entirely on to Him, which is the only possible act of faith. — NKW

What am I doing to try to earn God's favor? How am I learning to rest in what He has earned for me?

THE impossible is exactly what God does. The sure sign that we have no faith in God is that we have no faith in the supernatural. No man can believe God unless God is in him. The promises to Abraham are God all over from beginning to end. Don't only make room for God, but believe that God has room enough for you. — NKW

THERE are times when God seems to overlook certain forms of unbelief. At other times He brings our unbelief out suddenly into the light and makes us cringe with shame before it. It is not because He wants to show how miserable and mean we are, but because our particular form of un-faith is hindering the expression of His purpose in and through us.

— NKW

Where is my lack of faith most evident? How does it hinder God's purpose for me? For my family? For my church? For the world?

FAITH is not the means whereby we take God to ourselves; faith is the gift of God whereby He expresses His purposes through us.

— NKW

HEBREWS 11 impresses the life of faith over the life of human perfection. The first thing faith in God does is to remove all thought of relevant perfection. Some lives may seem humanly perfect and yet not be relevant to God and His purpose. — NKW

How are my attempts to perfect myself keeping me from being useful to God? Do I spend more energy pursuing what I want to achieve than I do in finding out what God wants me to believe?

IT is not what a man achieves, but what he believes and strives for that makes him noble and great. — NKW

THE story of Abraham does not close with his greatest act of faith, but goes on to record his progress to a sanctified life. Human nature likes to hear about the extraordinary, not the ordinary. It takes the Divine nature to be interested in grass and sparrows and trees because God made them. God's order is in nature; the devil's is in the spectacular.   — NKW

Do I live like an addict, always looking for my next religious "high," or like a saint, always willing to take the next step toward spiritual heights? Do I behave like God's audience, always waiting for His next spectacular stunt, or like a member of His team, always ready for my next turn to play?

MOST of us are pagans in a crisis; only one out of a hundred is daring enough to bank his faith in the character of God.   — SSM

BEWARE of making a fetish of consistency to convictions instead of developing your faith in God. Whenever we take what God has done and put it in the place of Himself, we instantly become idolaters. — NKW

Which of my convictions are more important to me than God? Considering the way I talk and behave, how might others answer this question for me?

FAITH for my deliverance is not faith in God. Faith means, whether I am visibly delivered or not, I will stick to my belief that God is love. There are some things learned only in a fiery furnace. — RTR

SPIRITUAL character is only made by standing loyal to God's character no matter what distress the trial of faith brings. The distress and agony the prophets experienced was the agony of believing God when everything that was happening contradicted what they proclaimed Him to be; there was nothing to prove that God was just and true, but everything to prove the opposite.   — OPG

Am I willing to lose my own
honor for the sake of God's? If I am
humiliated before friends and family
am I willing to accept it
as from God?

THE trial of faith is never without the essentials of temptation. It is to be questioned whether any child of God ever gets through the trial of his faith without at some stage being honor-stricken; what God does comes as a stinging blow, and he feels the suffering is not deserved, yet, like Job, he will neither listen to nor tell lies about God.   — OPG

WE say many things which we believe, but they have never been tested. Discipline has to come through all the things we believe in order to turn them into real spiritual possessions. It is the trial of our faith that is precious. It is heroism to believe in God.　　— PH

Which is better: a God who gives me what I want or a God who wants to give me what is good? If I could comprehend the privilege of existing in God's consciousness, how would my attitude about what I have and don't have change?

THE thing that is precious in the sight of God is faith that has been tried. Tried faith is spendable; it is so much wealth stored up in heaven, and the more we go through the trial of our faith, the wealthier we become in the heavenly regions.　　— PH

OUR faith must be built on the reality of being taken up into God's consciousness in Christ, not on our taking God into our consciousness. This means entering into a relationship with God whereby our will becomes one with the will of God. — PH

Are my desires becoming more like God's or less like them? Is my will moving closer to God's will or further away? What is my biggest area of disagreement with God? What do I fear losing if I would move over to His side?

CHRISTIANITY is not my consciousness of God, but God's consciousness of me. We must build our faith on the reality that we are taken up into God's consciousness in Christ, not that we take God into our consciousness. — PH

MODERN Christians make the mistake of thinking that we must plow the field, sow the seed, and reap the harvest in half an hour. If everything does not happen at once, we lose faith. Our Lord was never in a hurry with the disciples. He kept on sowing the seed whether or not He reaped their understanding.   — SHL

What seeds of righteousness has God sown in my life? How do I trample them in my attempts to get Him to sow something "prettier"? Do I have the faith to believe that God will increase whatever crop He sows? Do I have the grace to rejoice when others reap what I have sown?

JESUS spoke the truth of God, and by His own life produced the right atmosphere for it to grow, and then in faith left it alone, because He knew that the seed had in it all the germinating power of God and would bring forth fruit when placed in the right soil.   — SHL

JOB recognized . . . and maintained that in
the end everything would be explained and
made clear. His faith was not in a principle,
but in God, that He is just and true and right.

— BFB

*Is my faith strong enough to believe
that God is just when all around me
I see injustice? Can I believe that He
is true when He allows so many
people to twist His words to lie and
deceive? Can I believe that He is
right when science says He
is wrong?*

THE strength of Abraham's faith appears in that
he held to God's promise while he promptly
went to do what seemed to prevent its fulfil-
ment. He believed that God would fulfill all
He had promised and did not stay to question.

— NKW

To have faith tests us for all we are worth. We have to stand in the midst of a universe that is in conflict with the God whose character is revealed in Jesus Christ. Jesus Christ's statements reveal that God is a Being of love and justice and truth; the actual happenings in our circumstances seem to prove He is not. Are we going to remain true to the revelation that God is good? Are we going to be true to His honor, whatever may happen? If we are, we shall find that God in His providence makes the two universes, the universe of revelation and the universe of common sense, work in perfect harmony. — SSM

Am I willing to admit that my idea of goodness may be in conflict with what God says is good? Am I willing to admit that God is right?

Personal holiness is an effect, not a cause, and if we place our faith in human goodness, in the effect of Redemption, we shall go under when the test comes. — MUHH

THE great point of Abraham's faith in God was that he was prepared to do anything for God. Mark the difference between that and doing anything to prove your love to God.

— NKW

Are my spiritual acts more often an effort to get God to love me, an attempt to prove I love God, or an honest expression of my love for Him? Which does God prefer? Which do I prefer from the people I love?

IF there is only one strand of faith among all the corruption within us, God will take hold of that one strand.

— NKW

Faith Is Believing
What God Says
About the Son

OUR faith is in a Person Who is not deceived in anything He says or in the way He looks at things. Christianity is personal, passionate devotion to Jesus Christ as God manifest in the flesh. — FR

In what ways is my faith more like fate? Do I just give in passively to the way things are, or do I engage passionately with the One who gives meaning to everything that is?

FATE means stoical resignation to an unknown force. Faith is committal to One Whose character we do know because it has been revealed to us in Jesus Christ. — NKW

THE life of faith is to believe that Jesus Christ is not a fraud. The biggest fear a man has is never fear for himself but fear that his Hero won't get through; that He won't be able to explain things satisfactorily; for instance, why there should be war and disease. The problems of life get hold of a man and make it difficult for him to know whether in the face of these things he really is confident in Jesus Christ. The attitude of a believer must be, "Things do look black, but I believe Him; and when the whole thing is told I am confident my belief will be justified and God will be revealed as a God of love and justice."   — FR

Do I believe God with my head only or also with my heart? Do I believe Him enough to trust Him with my fears and failures? Do I believe Him enough to stop making excuses for my sin?

FAITH is the whole man rightly related to God by the power of the Spirit of Jesus.   — PF

WHAT counts in a man's life is the disposition that rules him. When God begins His work in us He does not make a mighty difference in our external lives, but He shifts the center of our confidence; instead of relying on ourselves and other people, we rely on God, and are kept in perfect peace.   — FR

Is the peace of Jesus present in
my life even when I m involved in
conflict? Is the joy of Jesus evident
in my life even when the pressures of
the world threaten to crush me?

THE Great Life is not that we believe *for* something, but that when we are up against things in circumstances or in our own disposition, we stake our all on Jesus Christ's honor. If we have faith only in what we experience of salvation, we will get depressed and morbid; but to be a believer in Jesus Christ is to have an irrepressible belief and a life of uncrushable joy.   — FR

To be a believer in Jesus Christ means we are committed to His way of looking at everything, not that we are open to discuss what people say He taught; that is the way difficulties have arisen with regard to Christian faith. Theology ought to be discussed; it does not follow, however, that our faith is assailed, but that in the meantime we stake our all in Jesus Christ.

— FR

What areas of my life are not yet in agreement with the life and words of Jesus? How do my disagreements with Jesus affect my life and the lives of those around me?

THE great lodestar of our life is — "I believe in Jesus Christ, and in everything on which I form an opinion I make room for Him and find out His attitude."

— FR

JESUS Christ did not come to us in the character of a celestial lecturer; He came to re-create us, to re-make us according to God's original plan, eternal lovers of God Himself, not absorbed into God, but part of the great Spirit-baptized humanity — "till we all come to the unity of the faith and of the knowledge of the Son of God, to a perfect man, to the measure of the stature of the fullness of Christ" (Ephesians 4:13).   — BE

How am I participating with God in His work of making me perfect? How am I resisting? Am I eager or reluctant to have God work out His purpose in and through my life?

WE take our faith much too lightly and think of our sanctification much too cheaply. We ought to rejoice when a man is saved, but remember what it cost God to make His grace a free gift. It cost agony we cannot begin to understand.   — BSG

WE must remind ourselves of the fundamental matters of our Christian relationship, that is, that in a Christian, faith and common sense are molded in one person by devotion to the mastership of Jesus Christ. This necessitates not conscious adherence to principles, but concentrated obedience to the Master.

— CD

Does my faith produce fanaticism or enthusiasm? Apathy or energy? Complacency or creativity? How is the person and passion of Jesus being revealed in and through me?

FAITH does not become its own object; that produces fanaticism. But it becomes the means whereby God unveils His purposes to us (Romans 12:2).

— CD

FAITH must be tested because only through conflict can head faith be turned into a personal possession. Faith according to Jesus must have its object real, no one can worship an ideal. We cannot have faith in God unless we know Him in Jesus Christ. God is a mere abstraction to our outlook until we see Him in Jesus and hear Him say, "He who has seen Me has seen the Father" (John 14:9). Then we have something to build upon, and faith becomes boundless.   — PF

How is God using conflict to take my faith from the superficial level of a nice idea to the deeper level of rock-solid reality?

TRUTH is a Person, not a proposition; if I pin my faith to a logical creed I will be disloyal to the Lord Jesus.   — DI

THINK of the things you are trying to have faith for! Stop thinking of them and think about your state in God through receiving Christ Jesus; see how God has enabled you to walk where you used to totter, and see what marvelous strength you have in Him. All the great blessings of God are ours not because we obey, but because we have put ourselves into a right relationship with God by receiving Christ Jesus the Lord, and we obey spontaneously.

— GW

Is my obedience a spontaneous response to God's love or a calculated effort to earn it? Do I work to earn God's blessing or rest to receive His love?

AS we look back we find that every time we have been blessed it was not through mechanical obedience, but by receiving from Jesus something that enabled us to obey without knowing it and life was flooded with the power of God.

— GW

WHEN you come to work for Jesus Christ, always ask yourself, Am I as confident in His power as He is in His own? If you deal with people without any faith in Jesus Christ it will crush the very life out of you. If we believe in Jesus Christ, we can face every problem the world holds.

— HG

What problem is the world facing due to people's lack of faith? Where might God want me to sow seeds of faith today?

UNTIL we know Jesus, God is a mere abstraction, and we cannot have faith in Him; but immediately upon hearing Jesus say, "He who has seen Me has seen the Father," we have something that is real, and faith is boundless. Faith is the whole man rightly related to God by the power of the Spirit of Jesus Christ.

— MUHH

IF Jesus Christ were manifested now, would we be like Him? Or would we have a hundred and one things to do before we could be as He is? We have not been taking time to purify ourselves as He is pure because we have been restless and annoyed; we have imagined that we have things to do that no one can do but ourselves. — LG

Which word better describes my condition: restless or restful? What am I trying to do for God that He has not assigned to me?

WE have no business to get into circumstances God does not put us into. Faith means keeping absolutely specklessly right with God; He does all the rest. — LG

To experience the loss of my own goodness is to enter into communion with God through Christ. If I try to be right, it is a sure sign I am wrong; the only way to be right is to stop trying to be right and to remain steadfast in faith in Jesus Christ.

— GW

Am I humble enough to admit when
I am wrong? Would I rather be
perceived as right by my friends
or as righteous by God?

WE are only what we are in the dark; all the rest is reputation. What God looks at is what we are in the dark — the imaginations of our minds; the thoughts of our hearts; the habits of our bodies; these are the things that mark us in God's sight.

— LG

IT is significant that Jesus Christ never says anywhere what modern evangelists say — "Believe certain things about Jesus Christ." Jesus says, "Believe also in Me" (John 14:1). In other words, "leave the whole thing to Me, you have nothing to do with anything but your actual life, the thing that lies nearest. It is gloriously uncertain how I will come in, but I will come."   — LG

What is the most surprising thing Jesus has done in my life? How has it changed what I believe about Him? What is the best thing Jesus has done in my life? Have I spent His blessing on myself or used it to bless others?

THE greatest thing in our lives is to remain loyal to Jesus, and this will evidence itself as His love at work in us.   — LG

WHEN once we see Jesus, He does the impossible thing as naturally as breathing. Our agony comes through the willful stupidity of our own heart. We won't believe, we won't cut the shore line, we prefer to worry on.

— MUHH

What comfort do I find in worrying? What is the worst that could happen if I stopped? What feeling does it give me that I refuse to give up?

JESUS Christ hits desperately hard at every one of the institutions we bank all our faith on naturally. The sense of property and of insurance is one of the greatest hindrances to development in the spiritual life. You cannot lay up for a rainy day if you are trusting Jesus Christ.

— SSM

THINK Who the New Testament says that Jesus Christ is, and then think of the despicable meanness of the miserable faith we have — "I haven't had this and that experience!" Think what faith in Jesus Christ claims — that He can present us faultless before the throne of God, unutterably pure, absolutely rectified, and profoundly justified. — MUHH

Am I allowing Jesus to make me into a citizen fit for heaven, or am I spending all His resources trying to make myself fit in better on earth?

WE are invited and commanded by God to believe that we can be made one with Jesus as He is one with God, so that His patience, His holiness, His purity, His gentleness, His prayerfulness are made ours. — OBH

THE way the gift of faith works in us and becomes real is by hearing. We first hear, and then we begin to trust. It is so simple that most of us miss the way. The way to have faith in the gospel of God's grace, in its deepest profundity as well as in its first working, is by listening to it. — OBH

Where do I expect faith to come from? Do I listen and obey so Jesus can manifest His faith in me. Or do I try to manufacture faith by combining experience and emotion?

THE holiness of Jesus is imparted as a sovereign gift of God's grace. We cannot earn it, we cannot pray it down, but, thank God, we can take it by faith, "through faith in his blood" (Romans 3:25 KJV). — OBH

To believe is literally to commit. Belief is a moral act, and Jesus makes an enormous demand of a man when He asks him to believe in Him. To be a believer in Jesus means to bank our confidence in Him, to stake our soul upon His honor. Many of us use religious jargon, we talk about believing in God, but our actual life proves that we do not really believe one-tenth of what we profess. — PH

In what ways does my life prove or disprove what I say I believe about Jesus?

THE peculiar aspect of religious faith is that it is faith in a person who relates us to Himself and commits us to His point of view, not faith in a point of view divorced from relationship to a Person. When through His Redemption we become rightly related to Him personally, our hearts are unshakeably confident in Him. That is the Divine anticipation — the tremendous work of God's supernatural grace being manifested in our mortal flesh. — PF

IN the past, the error of the Christian faith was that it paid no attention to a man's actual life. The present error is that humanity utilizes Christianity; if Jesus Christ does not coincide with our line of things, we toss Him overboard. Humanity is on the throne. In the New Testament the point of view is God and Man in union.

— SA

In what areas is my life out of align with Jesus? In what areas am I still trying to get Jesus to align Himself with me?

THE new birth will bring us to the place where spirit, soul, and body are identified with Christ, sanctified here and now and preserved in that condition, not by intuitions now, not by sudden impulses and marvelous workings of the new life within, but by a conscious, superior, moral integrity, transfigured through and through by our union with God through the Atonement.

— BP

IN any work I do for God, is my motive loyalty to Jesus, or do I have to stop and wonder where He comes in? If I work for God because I know it brings me the good opinion of those whose good opinion I wish to have, I am a Sadducee. The one great thing is to maintain a spiritual life which is absolutely true to Jesus Christ and to the faith of Jesus Christ.   — HG

How does my loyalty to another person, organization, or idea interfere with my loyalty to Jesus? How many of my "spiritual acts of service" are nothing more than an attempt to gain a good reputation or to get a tax decuction?

THE faith of Jesus is exhibited in His temptation and can be summed up in His own words: "I have come down from heaven, not to do My own will, but the will of Him who sent Me" (John 6:38). Jesus remained steadfastly loyal to His Father, and the saint has to keep the faith of Jesus.   — SHL

WE get in contact with the revelation facts of God's universe by faith wrought in us by the Spirit of God. Then as we develop in understanding, the two universes are slowly made one in us. They never agree outside Jesus Christ.

— SSM

How does my belief in Jesus make me more compatible with other aspects of His creation? Do I do more to desecrate the original order of God's creation or to restore it? Does my faith make a big difference, a little difference, or no difference in the world?

OUR Lord did not rebuke His disciples for making mistakes, but for not having faith. The two things that astonished Him were "little faith" and "great faith." Faith is not in what Jesus Christ can do, but in Himself.

— LG

THE essence of true religious faith is devotion to a Person. Beware of sticking to convictions instead of to Christ; convictions are simply the clothes of your growing life.   — NKW

Does my faith cleanse me superficially like a shower running over my body or does it purify me like blood running through my veins? How often do I settle for the appearance of Christianity rather than the authenticity of Christ?

THE Christian faith must stand in an Almighty Christ, not in a human being who became Divine.   — PR

Beware of worshiping Jesus as the Son of God, and professing your faith in Him as the Savior of the world, while you blaspheme Him by the complete evidence in your daily life that He is powerless to do anything in and through you. — DI

In which area of my life do I blaspheme Jesus by behaving as if He has no power over it? What keeps me from allowing Him to exercise power in this area? How might this sin be keeping others in darkness?

Are we banking in unshaken faith on the Redemption, or do we allow sin and wrong to obliterate Jesus Christ's power to save? We have to be so faithful to God that through us may come the awakening of those who have not yet realized that they are redeemed. — CHI

OUR unbelief stands as the supreme barrier to Jesus Christ's work in the souls of others. "He did not do many mighty works there because of their unbelief" (Matthew 13:58). But once I get over my own slowness to believe in Jesus Christ's power to save I become a real generator of His power to others. — CHI

Do I consider my unbelief a cute personality quirk or a serious spiritual defect? How do I damage others by making room in my life for unbelief? Do I place more faith in my church than I do in Jesus?

THE average man is inarticulate about his belief, and he does not connect his belief in goodness and truth and justice with Jesus Christ and the church because churches misrepresent Jesus Christ. We cannot corner God or the spiritual life. To think we can is the curse of denominational belief. — LG

Faith Is Believing

What God Says

About the Holy Spirit

WE can never tell how we shall have to decide in certain circumstances, but we have to see that we stand fast in the faith. We know what "the faith" is when we have gone through with God in any particular. "The faith" is faith in the Redemption and in the indwelling Spirit of God; faith that God is love, and that He will see us through if we stand steadfast to our confidence in Him.   — FR

*Do I trust God in the small
things, over which I have the
illusion of control, or just in the big
things, which I know I am powerless
to change or fix? Which is the
bigger expression of faith?*

IT is easy to stand fast in the big things, but very difficult in the small things.   — FR

WHEN the Spirit is at work in a time of mighty revival it is very difficult not to yield, but it is quite another thing to receive Him. If we yield to the power of the Spirit in a time of revival we may feel amazingly blessed, but if we do not receive the Spirit we are left decidedly worse and not better. — BE

Does my life demonstrate the Spirit and power of the Lord when I am angry and frustrated or only when I am happy and comfortable? Am I letting the Holy Spirit have His way in my thoughts, feelings, and actions?

THE Spirit of God is the One Who makes the simple act of faith the supernatural work of God. — OBH

ONE of the greatest disciplines in spiritual life is the darkness that comes not on account of sin, but because the Spirit of God is leading you from walking in the light of your conscience to walking in the light of the Lord. Defenders of the faith are inclined to be bitter until they learn to walk in the light of the Lord. Once we learn to walk in the light of the Lord, bitterness and contention are impossible.

— BP

Do I assume that only light, never darkness, comes from God? If that is so, why would God have bothered to make the night?

IN the Bible, clouds are always connected with God. Clouds are those sorrows or sufferings without or within our personal lives which seem to dispute the empire of God. Seen apart from God, the clouds or difficulties are accidents, but when seen as from the Spirit of God they become our teachers which show us how to walk by faith.

— GW

BY the power of the indwelling Holy Spirit we can bring every thought into captivity to the obedience of Christ, and can keep this body the chaste temple of the Holy Ghost. But are we doing it? By the power of the Holy Spirit we can keep our communications with other people the exact expression of what God is working in us. But are we doing it? The proof that we have a healthy vigorous faith is that we are expressing it in our lives and bearing testimony with our lips as to how it came about. — PF

Is my life set apart for use by God?
Do I use my body to do holy
things? Do I use my mouth
to speak holy words?

THE only holiness there is is the holiness derived through faith, and faith is the instrument the Holy Spirit uses to organize us into Christ. But do not let us be vague here. Holiness, like sin, is a disposition, not a series of acts. — PF

THE thought is full of unspeakable glory —
that God the Holy Ghost can come into my
heart and fill it so full that the life of God will
manifest itself all through this body which
used to manifest exactly the opposite. If I am
willing and determined to keep in the light
and obey the Spirit, then the characteristics of
the indwelling Christ will manifest themselves.

— BP

*Is my life characterized more
by light or by darkness? In what
ways does the Holy Spirit manifest
God's love through me? What am I
learning about God that the Holy
Spirit wants to express through
my life?*

UNTIL we know God, we have no faith.

— GW

FAITH is the indefinable certainty of God behind everything, and is the one thing the Spirit of God makes clearer and clearer as we go on. Do we know anything about confidence in God, or are we always hunting in our theological "wardrobes" for definitions?

— HSGM

Is my faith in God's goodness so confident that I am willing to let God's Spirit tell me the truth about myself?

FAITH means implicit confidence in Jesus, and that requires not intellect only but a moral giving over of myself to Him. How many have really received from God the Spirit that ruled Jesus Christ and which kept His spirit, soul, and body in harmony with God? The Holy Spirit will bring conviction of sin, He will reveal Jesus Christ, and He will bring in the power.

— FR

THE most formidable enemy to faith in God is rationalism. When people go down spiritually it is because they have begun to heed the earnestness which quotes the words of God without His Spirit. The first thing always that blinds us is that people are in earnest. — IS

Do I believe that God's plans are better than mine, His purposes higher, and His love superior? Am I mature enough in my faith to know what is best? Am I strong enough to choose it? Am I courageous enough to live it?

SOMETIMES we crave something less than the best. Beware! We ought to love the most what is best. The Spirit of God in us can teach us how to love the best, through faith, through knowledge, through everything until we are altogether in love with God, in absolute harmony with Him, absorbed in the one great purpose of God. — IYWB

HOW much of faith, hope, and love is worked in us when we try to convince somebody else? It is not our business to convince other people; that is the insistence of a merely intellectual, unspiritual life. The Spirit of God will do the convicting when we are in the relationship where we simply convey God's word.

— IYWB

Do I convey God's Word only through my lips or also through my life? Is my life a thoroughfare for God or a dead end?

THE faith that is the creation of God's Spirit in the human soul is never private and personal. When once that faith is created we are caught up into the terrific universal purpose of God. The Holy Spirit destroys our personal private life and turns it into a thoroughfare for God.

— NKW

IMAGINATION is the greatest gift God has given us, and it ought to be devoted entirely to Him. If you have been bringing every thought into captivity to the obedience of Christ, it will be one of the greatest assets to faith when the time of trial comes, because your faith and the Spirit of God will work together. — MUHH

Is my imagination stayed on God or Satan? Is it being fed by God or starved by Satan?

LEARN to associate ideas worthy of God with all that happens in Nature — the sunrises and the sunsets, the sun and the stars, the changing seasons. Then your imagination will never be at the mercy of your impulses, but will always be at the service of God. — MUHH

RELIGIOUS enterprise that has not learned to rely on the Holy Spirit makes everything depend on the human intellect — "God has said so-and-so. Now believe it and all will be right." But it won't. The basis of Jesus Christ's religion is the acceptance of a new Spirit, not a new creed, and the first thing the Holy Spirit does is to awaken us out of sleep. — BE

Am I sleeping in the false security of religion or resting in the safety of my relationship with Jesus?

ALL our efforts to pump up faith in the word of God is without quickening, without illumination. You reason to yourself and say, "Now God says this and I am going to believe it," and you believe it, and re-believe it, and re-re-believe it, and nothing happens, simply because the vital power that makes the words living is not there. We have to learn to rely on the Holy Spirit because He alone gives the Word of God life. — BE

THE Spirit of God always comes in surprising ways — "The wind blows where it wishes, and you hear the sound of it, but cannot tell where it comes from and where it goes. So is everyone who is born of the Spirit" (John 3:8).

— BE

Do I believe that God must work in other people's lives the same way He has worked in mine? Am I so insecure in my relationship with God that the only way for Him to validate my experience is by repeating it in someone else?

WE must keep in touch with God by faith, and see that we give others the same freedom and liberty that God gives us.   — MFL

DOCTRINES of faith are the explanation of how Jesus Christ makes us saints, but all the doctrine under heaven will never make a saint. The only thing that will make a saint is the Holy Ghost working in us what Jesus Christ did in the Atonement. Jesus Christ demands absolute devotion to Himself personally, then the application of His principles to our lives. For what purpose? That we may understand Him better. To be devoted to doctrines will twist us away from the Center; devotion to Jesus Christ relates our doctrines to the one Center, Jesus Christ. Read the words of the Spirit to the Church in Ephesus — "Nevertheless I have this against you, that you have left your first love. Remember therefore from where you have fallen; repent and do the first works, or else I will come to you quickly and remove your lampstand from its place — unless you repent" (Revelation 2:4–5).   — BSG

SUBJECT INDEX

SELECTION INDEX

Scripture Index

NOTE TO THE READER

The publisher invites you to share your response to the message of this book by writing Discovery House Publishers, Box 3566, Grand Rapids, MI 49501, USA. For information about other Discovery House books, music, or videos, contact us at the same address or call 1-800-653-8333. Find us on the Internet at http://www.dhp.org/ or send e-mail to books@dhp.org.